W9-CCD-010

STICK & LEARN
Woof!

BABY *animals*

TOP THAT™

Licensed exclusively to Top That Publishing Ltd
Tide Mill Way, Woodbridge, Suffolk, IP12 1AP, UK
www.topthatpublishing.com
Manufactured in Zhejiang, China

Woof!

The **puppy** wants to **play.**

It loves to **run,** **tumble,** and **chew!**

Find a **puppy** and a **ball. Stick** them with the other puppy, so they can have **fun!**

Woof!
Woof!
Woof!

ball

puppy

Puppies born to a **mommy** dog all at one time are called a **litter.**

Find the sticker!

Meow!

The **kitten** loves to **play** with a **ball** of yarn.

Playing makes it **strong!**

Find a **ball of yarn** and **stick** it where the kitten can **play** with it.

Meow!
Meow!
Meow!

yarn

kitten

Kittens **grow** quickly.
They start to explore
when they are about
two weeks old.

Find the sticker!

nibble!

The **baby rabbit** is exploring.

It loves to **nibble** tasty **grass**.

Find **one baby rabbit** and a **carrot. Stick** them on the **grass**.

nibble! Twitch! nibble!

rabbit

carrot

A baby rabbit is called a **kitten.** Kittens are born with their **eyes closed** and without fur.

Find the sticker!

Splash!

The **sea otter pup** is getting a ride from **mommy!**

She fluffs his fur so he will **float!**

Find **two sea otter pups** and **stick** them in the **water**.

Splash! Splash! Splash!

sea otters

seaweed

Mommy wraps her pup in **seaweed** to stop it floating away! **Bob! Bob!**

Find the sticker!

Waddle!

The **penguin chick** is looking for its **daddy!**

There he is!

Find the **penguin chick** and **stick** it with its **daddy.**

Waddle!

Waddle!

Waddle!

penguin

chick

Penguins hunt **underwater.** It is months before a chick is ready for its **first swim. Splash!**

Find the sticker!

Swing!

The **baby gorilla** loves to **climb** and **swing.**

Playing in the jungle is **fun!**

Find the **mommy gorilla** and **stick** her with her **baby.**

Swing!

Swing!

Swing!

gorilla

Baby gorillas can **crawl** at **two months** old and walk at **eight months** old.

Find the sticker!

Growl!

The **lion cub** loves to **play** rough and tumble.

Mommy doesn't mind!

Find two more **lion cubs** and **stick** them where they can **play** too!

Growl! Growl! Growl!

lioness

lion cub

A mommy lion is called a **lioness.** Look how she **carries** her cub!

Find the sticker!

Trumpet!

The **elephant calf** loves his **mommy.**

One day he will be as **big** as **her!**

Find an **elephant calf** and **stick** it next to its **mommy.**

Trumpet! Trumpet! Trumpet!

elephant

trunk

calf

Baby elephants **suck** their **trunks** like human babies suck their thumbs!

Find the sticker!

Yawn!

The **seal pup** is getting ready for its **first swim.**

Maybe **not today!**

Find a **seal pup** and **stick** it on the **beach,** so it can relax.

Yawn! Snooze! Yawn!

seal pup

beach

Seal pups are born on **land.** They grow up to be great **swimmers.**

Find the sticker!

Slide!

The **polar bear cub** is sliding on the **snow!**

She wants her **brother** to **join in!**

Find another **polar bear cub** and **stick** him with his **sister.**

Slide!

Slip!

Slide!

snow

polar bear cub

Cubs are born in a **den** under the snow. After a few months they **explore** outside.

Find the sticker!

Bleat!

The **fawn** is learning to **walk.**

Its legs are still a bit **wobbly!**

Find a big **mommy deer** and **stick** her with her little **fawn.**

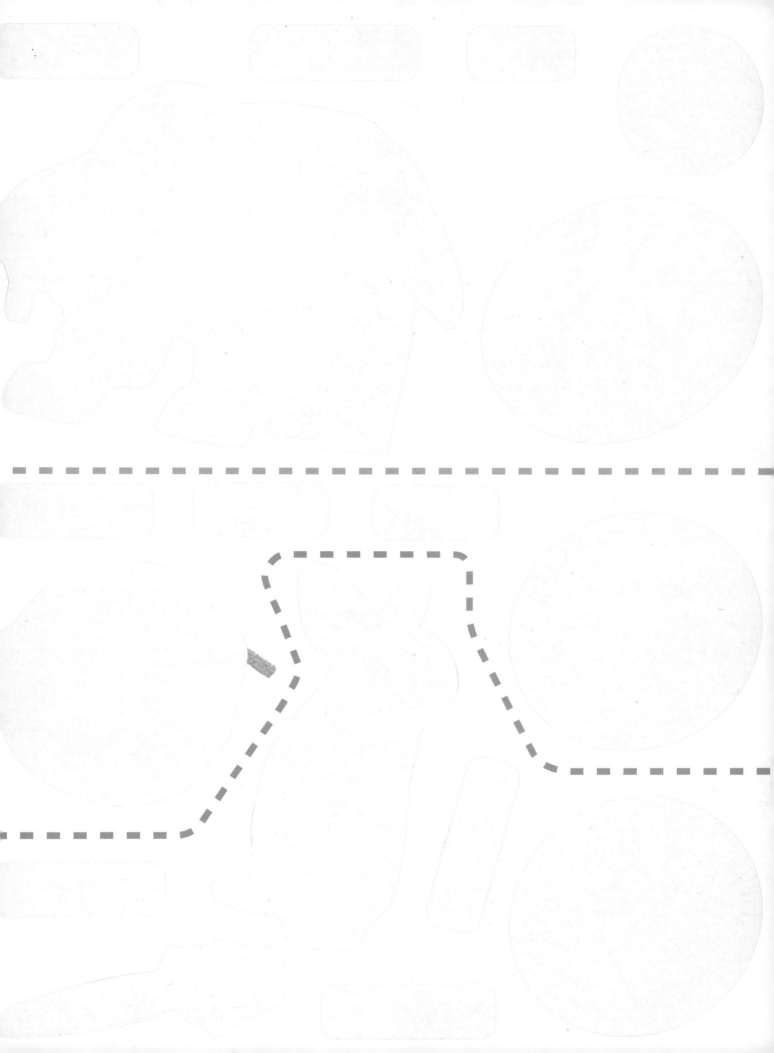

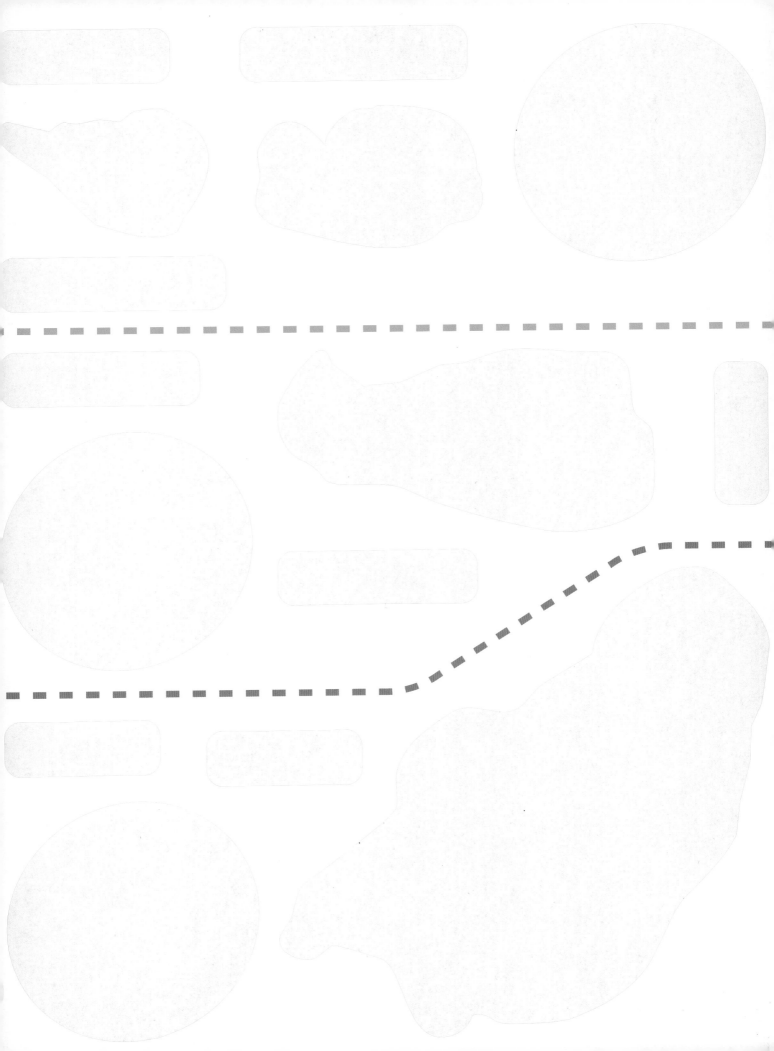

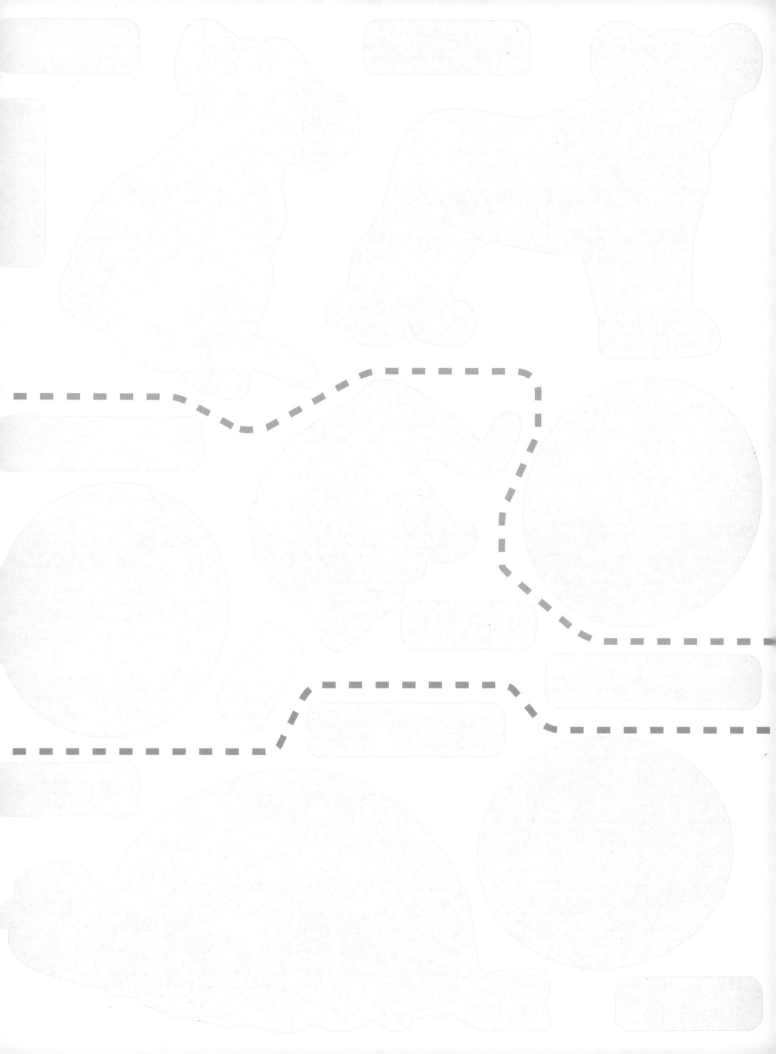

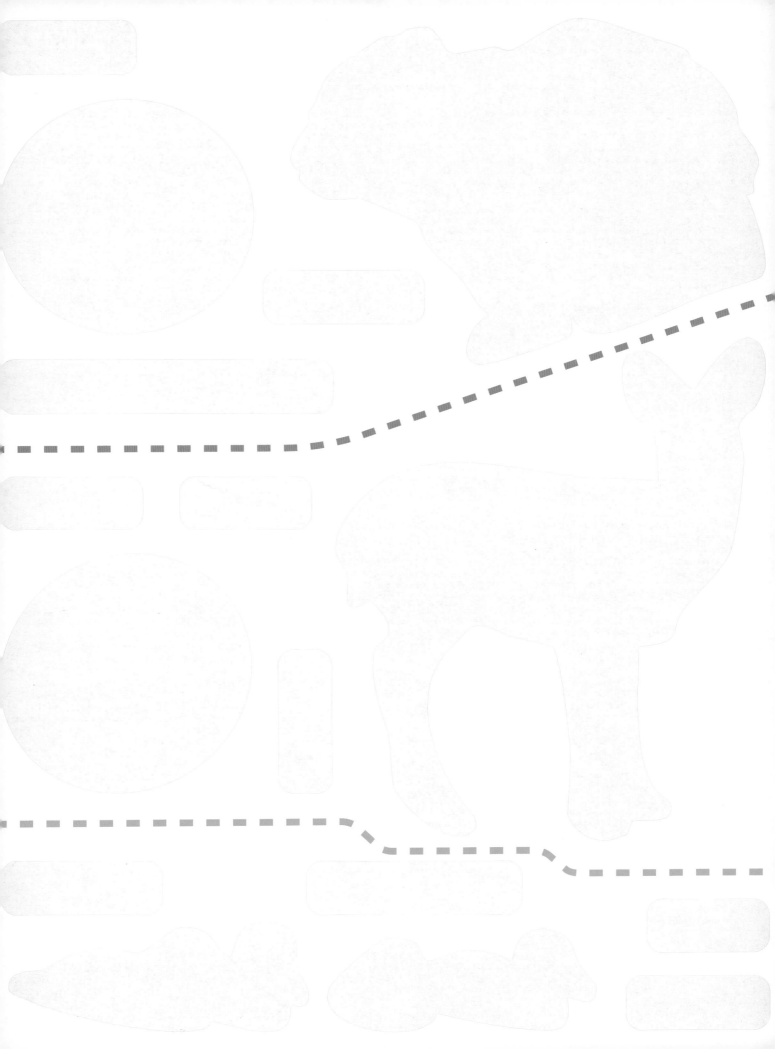

Use these stickers in this book.

Use these stickers anywhere you like.

Use these stickers anywhere you like.